VULTURES
& CONDORS

First published in Great Britain in 2001 by
Colin Baxter Photography Ltd
Grantown-on-Spey
PH26 3NA
Scotland
www.worldlifelibrary.co.uk

WorldLife Library Series

A CIP Catalogue record for this book is available from the British Library.

ISBN 1-84107-072-6

Photographs © 2001

Printed in China

VULTURES & CONDORS

David Houston

Colin Baxter Photography Ltd, Grantown-on-Spey, Scotland

Contents

A Scavenging Way of Life

'These disgusting birds, with their bald, scarlet heads, formed to revel in putridity'
Charles Darwin, *The Voyage of the Beagle*, 1832.

Vultures do not get a good press. Charles Darwin was clearly not impressed when he saw turkey vultures for the first time, in South America in 1832, during his exploration round the world recounted in *The Voyage of the Beagle*. Today when we mention vultures most people have a mental image of a group of macabre and grotesque birds who earn their living by circling a lion kill, hoping to snatch a few scraps from the carcass. Maybe being a hanger-on at predator kills is not a glamorous way of life. But it is also not a true picture.

Contrary to popular opinion, vultures do not get their food by stealing it from predators. Vultures are birds which feed on meat, just like any predator, but they do not kill. They rely instead on finding animals which are already dead. Some vulture species will indeed collect around predator kills, but these provide them with only a tiny amount of food, for the simple reason that most predators are not willing to give up their hard-won prey to a bunch of vultures, and will defend and guard their kills carefully. Vultures and condors feed mainly by finding animals which have died from some other cause. Far more animals die each year from diseases, parasites, starvation, old age, accidents, or any combination of these natural causes, than are ever killed by predators. Vultures specialize in finding such dead animals. They are supremely efficient as scavengers, and in many wildlife communities vultures are far more abundant than large predators, and will eat a greater amount of meat than all of the mammalian predators combined. Indeed, one can argue that vultures are perhaps the most successful of all birds of prey, for in those countries where they are found, and where they have not been

An Andean condor soars over the peaks of the Andes.

persecuted by man, they are often far more abundant than any other kind of raptor. This book looks at their way of life and the role that they play in wildlife communities.

We tend to regard the large mammal predators, such as wolves, lions or tigers, with respect and esteem. Their physical power is only a part of their attraction. These animals have developed, through natural selection, a range of adaptations which make them supremely efficient killers. Most people find the way they are designed as killing machines fascinating; from their camouflage which allows them to blend into the background to their complex hunting behavior and skill at tracking their prey. Their eventual food – meat – is exactly the same as the food taken by the despised vultures. But earning a living by being a scavenger is also a highly specialized way of life and has required the vultures to develop their own remarkable adaptations. The condors and other large vultures are among the most spectacular birds in the world. In this book we will consider just what adaptations are needed to be a good scavenger, and why it is among the birds rather than the mammals that the most successful type of scavenger has developed.

A pair of lappet-faced vultures.

There are 22 different species of vultures in the world, found in North and South America, Africa, Europe and Asia. Only Australia lacks vultures. The name 'condor' is given to the two most spectacular of the American vultures, the California and Andean condors. Their smaller relatives in America are all called

8

A young white-backed vulture prepares to land, lowering its feet ready for touchdown. In many savanna areas of Africa these birds are the commonest of all the vultures, sometimes collecting in groups of several hundred.

vultures, such as the turkey and black vultures. Curiously, these birds are not at all related to the scavenging birds found in the Old World, which are all called vultures, and which look similar to, and share the same way of life as, the American condors and vultures.

The vulture way of life is quite unique. Almost all meat-eating mammals are both predators and scavengers. Wolves or lions will usually kill to get their food, but they will not hesitate to scavenge a free meal if they ever chance upon a dead animal. None of these mammalian carnivores anywhere in the world is an exclusive scavenger which feeds only by finding carcasses. It is only among the birds, in the many species of vulture, that we find animals which can live exclusively by scavenging. This can be a risky way of life. If a vulture or condor is getting hungry, it cannot go out and kill something; it has to search, wait and hope that an animal will die conveniently close and provide it with a meal. As we shall see in the next chapter, all vultures and condors are descended from ancestors that at one time were predators and killed their own prey. Why did vultures abandon the ability to kill and devote themselves to a life of scavenging?

Whatever our views of the appearance of vultures when we see them close-up, most people would agree that when they are in the air they are among the most graceful and spectacular of all flying animals. They have a great mastery of soaring flight and rarely need to flap their wings. They rely on riding natural air currents to carry them the great distances they need to travel to find food. In *The Voyage of the Beagle*, Charles Darwin wrote of condors, 'It is truly wonderful and beautiful to see so great a bird, hour upon hour, without any apparent exertion, wheeling and gliding over mountain and river'.

As we shall see, it is their skill and efficiency in flight which is one of the reasons that has made vultures and condors so successful as scavengers.

A young Ruppell's griffon vulture from Africa.

Flight

Soaring effortlessly on their broad wings, condors and vultures have a real mastery of the air. Their speciality is soaring flight. Most birds fly by powered flight, where large breast muscles on the body of the bird provide the power for the wing beats, and these drive the bird through the air, and generate lift to keep it aloft. But this method of flying uses a great deal of energy. Soaring flight does not require the bird to flap its wings at all. The bird just holds its wings open and takes advantage of natural air currents to gain the energy to keep itself in the air.

Vultures have a skillful understanding of their environment that allows them to detect where there will be currents of rising air. Mountains and hills are an obvious source of lift, because any wind blowing over the land will be forced upwards whenever it reaches rising land, and if the birds position themselves along a slope or cliff they can remain within the zone of rising air. Provided that the air stream is rising faster than the birds themselves are sinking, overall they will gain in altitude. Air streams can also develop into a wave form after passing over a mountain or hill range, and these may provide areas of lift many miles downwind from the original obstruction. These 'standing waves' can reach very great altitudes – far higher than the original hill which started the wave in the air stream. We know vultures and condors can attain remarkable altitudes. The world altitude record for any bird is held by a Ruppell's griffon vulture which is alleged to have collided with a commercial aircraft at 37,000 ft (over 11,000 m). Many people doubt the accuracy of this extreme report, because at this altitude the air temperature would be around -58°F (-50°C). But there is no doubt that, even though they rarely flap their wings, vultures can achieve considerable heights.

In warm countries vultures specialize in the use of thermal upcurrents. These develop when the sun heats the ground, perhaps at a patch of bare soil or rock, and the heated area causes a patch of warm air to develop immediately above the ground. The warm air has a lower density than the surrounding slightly cooler air, and so eventually it will begin to rise. If the mass of warm air is large enough, as it rises from the ground it will break away as a large bubble, forming a swirling mass of dust called a 'dust devil', which develops a shape rather like a doughnut. The air circulates upwards in the middle and downwards on the outside. Vultures are highly skilled at locating these thermal upcurrents and positioning themselves so that they remain in the narrow central zone of rising air and avoid the surrounding areas of sinking air. They circle inside the thermal, rapidly gaining altitude. Once a vulture has gained height, it can glide away into still air, where it will slowly lose altitude all the time it is gliding until it is near the ground and will need to find another source of rising air and climb again. In Africa, vultures can climb up to 15,000 ft (4500 m) in strong thermals. They probably only use high altitude flight when traveling long distances. When foraging for food they fly at much lower altitudes so that they can search the ground for carrion.

This method of flying requires a special design of bird. A vulture needs to be able to glide through still air for a long distance, but to lose relatively little altitude while it is doing so. This requires a large wing area in relation to the size of the bird. However, the zone of rising air inside the core of a thermal is quite narrow, and so if a bird is to keep in the rising air and avoid the surrounding sinking air it must be able to turn tightly within a small circle and maneuver skillfully. Again, this ability is determined by the ratio of wing area to body weight. Colin Pennycuick has made major advances in our understanding of bird flight in general, and has been particularly interested in how vultures and condors fly. His studies have shown that the wing shape used by vultures is a compromise between several conflicting requirements. For the best soaring performance a vulture should have a large wing area that is a long and thin shape – rather like the wing shape found in an albatross or a man-made sailplane. But the problem with this design is that for a bird as large as a vulture, the wings would have to be so long that the bird would probably not be able to flap them at all on the ground when it needed to

Two Ruppell's griffon vultures fly out over the East African plains in search of food. Vultures not only use their excellent eyesight to spot carcasses on the ground, but also watch their neighbors flying nearby, and will quickly follow any other bird that they see descending to the ground.

The bearded vulture is a specialist scavenger that lives among the highest peaks of Old World mountain ranges such as the Alps, Himalayas and Pyrenees. It feeds particularly on the bones from animal carcasses, and is the only animal known to make bone the main part of its diet.

take off, and might have real problems landing in a tree without breaking its wings. So, instead, the vultures have their large surface area in the shape of a shorter, broader wing. This is not so aerodynamically efficient, but it is more practical.

Colin Pennycuick developed an exciting method to study the flight performance of vultures in East Africa, by following them in his sailplane, and comparing their flight performance and speed with that of his own craft. He found that when flying in still air a member of a large species such as a Ruppell's griffon vulture would travel about 200 ft (60 m) forward for every 3 ft (1 m) it lost in height. They averaged about 30 mph (50 kmph) in long-distance travel, which means that during the day a bird could easily search over many hundreds of miles. My own studies at the breeding colony of these birds showed that at some times in the year the birds were daily traveling about 90 miles (140 km) from the nest to reach the herds of wildebeest that provide them with most of their food. California condors also average around 30 mph (50 kmph), and one condor was recorded traveling 140 miles (225 km) in a day. Andean condors also travel as far as 125 miles (200 km) from their nests to find food. This means that the larger vultures cover vast areas of ground searching for food: Andean condors range over about 500 sq miles (1300 sq km), and African bearded vultures up to 925 sq miles (2400 sq km). Even the smaller American turkey vulture will range over up to 140 sq miles (360 sq km). Long-distance commuting is part of the normal way of life for many vultures.

We might expect that to be an efficient soaring bird a vulture would have to be as light in weight as possible. Surprisingly, this is not correct. Colin Pennycuick has shown that the speed with which a gliding bird flies is directly related to its weight. This is why some man-made sailplanes are built with watertanks, so they can deliberately increase their weight. To be able to travel fast, vultures and condors need to be heavy. Being a large bird has many other advantages for a scavenger. It makes them better able to drive off other scavengers, like coyotes or jackals, at a carcass, or compete with the other

vultures. It also allows them to eat a large amount of food at each meal – larger vultures can swallow the equivalent of about 20 per cent of their body weight. They can also store more fat, and so survive longer periods between meals – large vultures like a condor or griffon vulture can survive for many weeks without eating. For all these reasons, vultures have evolved into large birds and have generally developed as large a body size as the flying conditions in their habitat will allow.

Flying is a critical component of the way of life of a vulture, because soaring flight requires so very little energy – dramatically less than any other form of travel. Colin Pennycuick calculates that a vulture uses only slightly more energy when flying than when it is standing on the ground doing nothing. But if it were to use flapping flight it would use perhaps 30 times more energy. Being able to travel using little energy is extremely important for a scavenger. Large grazing mammals do not die very often, so food for vultures will be found infrequently. A bird will have to search over vast areas of land to find a meal. And, if a dead animal is around, there will be plenty of scavenging mammals who might find it first, so vultures have to be able to arrive quickly. A scavenger will only be able to survive if the amount of energy that it uses finding a meal is less than the energy it gains from eating that meal. In other words, to be a good scavenger you have to be able to travel cheap, and fast. Birds have a huge advantage over mammals in this respect. In terms of the amount of energy required to travel a given distance, for animals in general even powered flight is less expensive than either running or swimming. And, as we have seen, soaring flight requires infinitely less energy than powered flight.

Flying has many other advantages. Birds can spot carcasses easily from the air because they have a far better view of the surrounding countryside than a mammal on the ground, where trees and bushes interrupt the view. They can

American turkey vultures circle in a thermal.

travel much faster by flying than any mammal can by running, so they search a larger area of ground each day. They can also keep an eye on other vultures flying on the far horizon, and join them if they see any birds descending to the ground, which will probably lead to a meal. This method of finding food – watching the behavior of their neighbors – is used by virtually all vultures. These are all advantages that only birds have, because they can fly. This is why birds are far better scavengers than mammals. And it is probably why no mammal species has ever evolved as an exclusive scavenger, but so many birds have.

Finally, the dependence that vultures have on gliding flight is probably why they have become exclusive scavengers. All of the mammalian carnivores which scavenge are also predators. Vultures and condors are descended from ancestors which at one time were also predators. So at some stage in their evolution the vultures gave up the ability to kill. At first it is difficult to understand why they should have done this. It makes their lives far more precarious, because if they were to retain the ability to kill they would have a far wider range of potential food available to them. But in order to become scavengers they had to totally adapt to be highly efficient soaring fliers: only in this way could they travel the enormous distances necessary to find food, while using very little energy. This meant that they needed to develop a large body size and the wing shape needed for efficient soaring flight. But the consequences of this mean that vultures are not at all agile at slow flight speeds. To be a predator you need to be able to attack active prey, and this requires the ability to maneuver in the air, land accurately, and chase at low altitude near the ground. Vultures cannot do any of these things. They have had to abandon these skills because they were incompatible with developing the wing shape and body design needed for being an efficient long-distance soaring bird. So in order to totally adapt themselves to becoming scavengers they had to give up the skills needed to be a predator.

Vultures and Condors of the World

The evolution of large, scavenging birds is in many ways more closely tied to mammal evolution than to the evolution of other bird species. This is because it is grazing mammals like antelope, deer and cattle that provide vultures with their food. The mammals are an ancient line of animals, which date back to the late Triassic period about 220 million years ago. But this was the era of the dinosaurs, and for a long period of time mammals remained small, nocturnal and rather insignificant creatures. It was only with the extinction of the dinosaurs about 65 million years ago that the mammals began to thrive. Around this time the world environment was changing fast, new types of plants had been evolving, and in particular grasslands were soon to spread over the world for the first time. This provided a new food for mammals, and a great range of plant-eating mammals which could graze on the new grasslands began to appear. The elephants are descended from one line of these first ungulates, but most of the other early forms died out. They were replaced about 40 to 55 million years ago by the more modern grazing mammals that dominate the world today. The first vultures appear in the fossil record around the same time, 40 to 50 million years ago. So the vultures are a very ancient line of birds, which evolved alongside the cattle, deer and antelope on which they fed.

At one time the different kinds of vultures were classified together in the scientific order Falconiformes, along with all the other birds of prey such as eagles and falcons. But as far back as 1876 the British zoologist Thomas Huxley had realized that the vultures from America were quite unlike those from Africa. He suggested they may not be related at all. There are many features of their anatomy and behavior which are different, and this has been confirmed by modern molecular classification techniques. Recent work by Michael Wink has

Two young Andean condors.

23

shown that there are probably three groups of vultures in the world which have evolved quite independently. The condors and the smaller American vultures are descended from the same line of ancestry as the storks and other water-birds. Many people now classify them alongside the storks in the order Ciconiiformes. Some modern storks, like the marabou, feed mainly by scavenging dead fish, meat and any other prey they can find, and it is easy to imagine such a line of storks developing into exclusively scavenging birds. Most of the vultures of the Old World, in Europe, Africa and Asia, however, are descended from the same ancestry as the birds of prey, such as eagles and buzzards, and belong in the Falconiformes. But two of the Old World vultures, the bearded and Egyptian, are so distinct from the other vultures that they probably come from a quite separate ancestry within the birds of prey. The vultures are a textbook example of what zoologists call 'convergent evolution' – that is, a group of animals which look very similar not because they are closely related but because they have independently developed a similar range of adaptations. If we were to find a mixed

Egyptian vulture.

group of vultures in a cage in a zoo, it would be difficult to see what separates the American from the Old World vultures, because they look so very similar. Vultures in America look like vultures in Africa because they have quite separately evolved the same features in order to be efficient scavengers, not because they are in any way related.

There are certain features of vultures, from whichever of the groups they come from, that we recognize and which make them characteristically distinct from all other large meat-eating birds. As well as relying on scavenging rather than killing, they usually have bare skin on the head and neck, which helps them to keep clean when feeding on messy carcasses. This is also important in their heat regulation because, as large birds often living in hot climates, they can have problems with overheating, and they use these bare skin areas to radiate heat away from the body and prevent thermal stress. They have weak feet, without the sharp talons that we find in raptors, because their feet are designed for walking rather than for killing prey. Vultures are usually large birds, and some species, such as the American condors and the Old World griffon vultures are among the heaviest birds in the world which can still fly. Vultures rely on soaring flight to a greater extent than any other type of land bird, and some of the larger species cannot really flap their wings or use powered flight for any great distance. They also show little sexual dimorphism, which means that in most species the male and female cannot be told apart by differences in size or plumage color. This is unusual among birds of prey, where the female is often larger than the male and has a more cryptic coloration. Vultures also tend to be rather silent birds. There may be a good reason for this, because when they are feeding they do not want to attract the attention of passing wolves or lions who might steal their food. The American vultures are unusual in not having a syrinx, which is the structure most birds use to produce song, and both Old and New World vultures make a weird range of hissing and wheezing noises rather than normal bird song.

The remarkable convergence of the vultures from their different lines of ancestry goes further than just these individual characteristics. In both the Old and New Worlds we usually find several species of vultures living together in the same area, to form scavenging guilds. A guild is a group of species which collect together at a carcass and collaborate in their feeding. Hans Kruuk carried out some of the first detailed studies on African vultures in the Serengeti in East Africa, and showed clearly that although up to six species of vulture may arrive together at a carcass, they are not directly competing with each other because

A group of African white-backed vultures gathering in a tree.
Like all griffon vultures, white-backs are very social, and often collect in groups like
this before or after feeding to preen, stretch their wings and rest.

each is specialized to take a different type of food from the carcass. Since Kruuk's study others have found similar guilds in all the other vulture communities in both the Old and New Worlds.

The guilds which have evolved are remarkably similar. In both the Old and New World we find large species, such as condors and griffon vultures, which are dull in coloration, travel huge distances when searching for food, collect in groups at carcasses and have long necks that enable them to reach into the meat and internal organs. Then there are medium-sized species, such as the king vulture in America and the white-headed and lappet-faced vultures in Africa, which are brightly colored, most often feed within a small foraging range, and usually do not collect in large numbers at a carcass. They specialize in feeding on the skin, tendons and tougher parts of the carcass. Then finally in both guilds there are small species, such as the American black and turkey vultures and the Old World Egyptian and hooded vultures. They travel large distances foraging, feed on a wide range of food items apart from the food they obtain from carcasses, and when they do feed alongside the larger vultures they specialize in taking small scraps of food the other birds leave, and picking the bones clean.

An American black vulture.

Different scavenging guilds have developed the same range of species, each specialized for feeding in a slightly different way. They have different bill shapes, different feet, and different body shapes so that each species takes a different type of food from the carcass.

American Condors and Vultures

Fossils of the first American vultures appear in the Eocene, about 40 to 50 million years ago, and they became extremely abundant when feeding among the rich mammal community that developed during the Pleistocene in North America. This community included some spectacular mammals that are no longer with us, such as two elephant species, the mastodon and mammoth, together with a great range of antelopes, giant sloths, camels, horses and peccaries. But the American vultures are also found as fossils in the Old World, and so at one time this group of birds lived all over the world.

There is a remarkable fossil site at La Brea tar pits, in the suburbs of Los Angeles. These pits date back to about 10,000 years ago, and consist of a series of tar sediments that lay at the bottom of waterholes. When grazing animals came to drink, many of them became trapped in the tar. The dying animals attracted in their turn predators and scavengers, including wolves, saber-toothed tigers, cheetahs and condors, who then themselves became trapped and preserved. Over half of all the fossil birds found in the asphalt deposits at La Brea are birds of prey, and vultures are particularly abundant. These fossil beds contain a number of relations of the modern California condor. *Teratornis merriami* had a wingspan up to 12 ft (3.7 m), slightly larger than the modern California condor whose wingspan reaches 10 ft (3 m). But this was tiny compared to a fossil teratorn species from Argentina, *Argentavis magnificens*, which may have been the largest flying bird of all time, with a wingspan approaching 23 ft (7 m). The American vultures were highly successful and gave rise to a large number of species, most of which are now extinct. This is because the mammals on which they depended also suffered a major extinction crisis.

At the end of the Pleistocene, only about 10,000 years ago, there was a

American turkey vultures have large nostrils and a good sense of smell.

dramatic extinction of about 67 different kinds of mammal that had been living in North America. Paul Martin first advanced the theory that this was caused by the first arrival of prehistoric man, who entered America through the land bridge across the Bering Sea from Russia, and as man spread south he hunted to extinction many of the large mammals that were found there. At the same time the climate was changing fast, and this may also have been a factor, but the result was that many vulture species died out along with the mammals they depended on. Today only seven species of New World vultures remain, from the great condors of the Andes and California to the smaller black and turkey vultures.

An adult male Andean condor.

As a group they share a number of strange characteristics with the storks, who are probably their closest relations. Most of these are technical features of their skulls and skeletons, but they also share some behaviors, such as squirting urine onto their legs to help them keep cool as the water evaporates, and which sometimes makes their legs look as if they have been whitewashed. American vultures are also curious in that they do not build nests, but usually lay their eggs on bare ground in rocky caves or hollow logs.

The most distinctive are the Andean and California condors. Both live in mountainous areas, and need strong upcurrents to keep them aloft. The California condor is the largest flying bird in North America with a wingspan of 9 or 10 ft (3 m), but at 8.5 kg (19 lb) not quite the heaviest – both the trumpeter swan and some male turkeys get slightly heavier. The California condor is now one of the rarest birds in the world and would

American black vultures are very sociable birds, and regularly collect in large groups at suitable feeding sites. This is one species which regularly associates with man, and can be found in large numbers in towns and cities in Central and South America feeding on garbage.

almost certainly be extinct had it not been for the massive conservation effort made in recent years (see pp.65-66). We know that at one time condors were found over much of North America, because fossils have been found from California across to Florida and as far north as New York. Originally they probably fed among the herds of large grazing animals that flourished before man arrived on the scene. Within more recent times there has been a continued decline in the numbers of the remaining wild ungulates which live on open grasslands. This removed the food supply for the condors, and now they are confined to a small area of mountains in California. There is remarkable archive film taken in the 1930s, when condors were more numerous, showing large groups of birds feeding together on a dead donkey. It looks remarkably like a scene from the African savannas. They probably did feed in a similar way to African griffon vultures, foraging over huge areas in search of dead animals, and collecting in groups whenever a carcass was located.

The Andean condor is slightly larger than the California condor, and is the only species of American vulture in which the male and female can be clearly distinguished – the male is larger and has a handsome crest on the head. Condors lived at one time along the whole of the Andes chain in South America, although this species has also suffered a severe contraction in its range in recent years. They are magnificent fliers, and search the mountains for dead vicuna, guanaco and domesticated llamas and alpaca. Jerry McGahan, who carried out one of the first studies on these birds in the wild in Colombia, found groups of up to 17 birds feeding together at the same carcass, although today this would be a rare sight. Some birds also breed in the mountains and travel over the coastal deserts to feed on the rich supply of dead whales, seals and other marine animals that wash up from the seas along the west coast of South America.

Among the smaller American vultures perhaps the most remarkable are the Cathartes vultures, of which there are three species, the turkey (which has four subspecies), the greater yellow-headed and the lesser yellow-headed. They differ only slightly in their wing and tail shape and in the color of their heads. We still know remarkably little about these common birds. The greater yellow-headed vulture was only discovered as recently as 1964 in the rainforests of South America. This might not be surprising if it were a small, cryptic little bird, but this is one of the most abundant, conspicuous and widely distributed birds in South American forests, and the fact that it had gone unnoticed indicates how little attention has been paid to vultures.

All these Cathartes vultures have a remarkable ability to locate food by smell. Most birds cannot smell well, but these vultures can. This was first demonstrated in some experiments carried out by Kenneth Stager, who had noted that the birds were often used by engineers to locate leaks in gas pipes, because the birds would fly in circles over the leaking gas, attracted by the smell which the gas company put into the gas – which happens to be a chemical also found in rotting meat. Whether vultures could or could not smell had been a controversial topic for many years. In 1826 James Audubon carried out some experiments. He placed out some foul-smelling rotting carcasses that were covered so that they could not be seen from the air. He noted that the vultures failed to find them, and concluded that vultures could not smell. But we now know that vultures have a highly developed sense of smell, with a large olfactory region in the brain, but that they do not like eating meat which is putrefying – which is no doubt why they failed to come down to Audubon's experiment. Normally vultures eat carcasses that are relatively fresh, and they will deliberately avoid meat that is old, probably because of the unpleasant bacteria toxins that will be present.

This ability to smell means that these vultures can live not only in open deserts and prairies, but also in dense forest. Indeed, the Amazon rainforest in South America holds large numbers of these birds. Tropical rainforest may seem an unlikely place to find vultures, and they can only survive there because of this ability to find their food by smell. In these forests, most of the plant-eating

mammals such as monkeys and sloths live in the tree canopy. Predators on these canopy mammals are rare, and most animals die from malnutrition or disease. These animals fall to the forest floor when they die, and in the heat of the humid tropics within a few hours they are giving off a slight smell that the birds can detect as they fly just above the tree canopy. The Cathartes vultures fly very low, immediately above the tree canopy, sniffing all the time. As soon as they detect the smell of carrion, they fly below the canopy and hop from branch to branch, following the direction where the scent is strongest, until they find their meal.

I have studied the remarkable abilities of these birds by placing out carcasses and seeing how long it takes for the vultures to find them – they usually do this within about a day. And they can find carcasses that are hidden by dried leaves just as quickly as visible carcasses. They have to be quick, because in the humid tropics a small carcass will be destroyed by maggots and other insect larvae within a few days. Vultures are the dominant meat-eating animals in the forests of South America. They can even find small carcasses, of rodents or small birds. But Cathartes vultures also forage over open habitats such as grasslands and deserts, and are the most successful of the American vultures. The turkey vulture is found over the southern half of North America as well, and some of these birds are migrants – millions of them travel down through Central America each fall to spend the winter in the tropics. In recent years turkey vultures have been extending their range further north in summer into North America, perhaps taking advantage of a ready food supply from animals run over on highways: these small roadside snacks are a convenient source of food.

The black vulture often feeds alongside turkey and yellow-headed vultures, but it lacks any sense of smell. When it is feeding in forest areas the only way it can find food under trees is to follow the Cathartes vultures and use them to lead it to food. But black vultures also live in open habitats, especially along rivers

Turkey vultures sunbathing in the early morning.

and low-lying swamp areas where they feed on stranded fish, hatchling turtles and many other foods. They are also the one American vulture which associates closely with man, and many cities in Central and South America have large numbers of these birds wandering the streets, cleaning up scraps at markets and garbage dumps, and generally acting as useful urban cleaners. There has been some fascinating research on the behavior of these birds by Patty Rabenold which has shown that they have a more complicated lifestyle than other vultures, and live in family groups which remain together and help each other to forage for food.

Finally, the most bizarre-looking of all the vultures is the king vulture from Central and South America. This wonderful bird has a head and neck colored with a complex pattern of oranges, pinks, and purples, and the weird effect is heightened by pendulous wattles and corrugating skin folds. It also has a striking black and white plumage, which makes it equally spectacular in flight with a distinctive pattern on the wings. King vultures are found in both forested areas and open country, and often congregate along with turkey, yellow-headed and black vultures. Because they are so much larger, and have powerful bills, they can tear the skin and open the carcasses of large mammals that smaller vultures cannot handle, and so king vultures are an important member of the scavenging guild and make food available to other vultures. Like the black vulture, the king vulture has no sense of smell, and has to use the Cathartes vultures to find food. We still know very little about the king vulture, but it is particularly vulnerable to forest disturbance, and in South America is usually only found in areas where the forests have healthy mammal populations. The black and king vultures tend to fly at high altitudes, from where they can keep an eye on the Cathartes vultures who fly at a lower altitude just above the tree canopy. Whenever they see vultures descending into the forest, they will come down to join them and so be led to food.

A young king vulture chick.

Old World Vultures

Like the American vultures, the Old World vulture group has an ancient fossil record and many species are known from the early Miocene, up to 26 million years ago – so the group must have originated some time before this. Fossils are found in many parts of America as well as the Old World, and these birds only died out in America about 10,000 years ago, with the Pleistocene extinctions that caused the demise of so many other animals.

I studied the African vultures in the Serengeti National Park in Tanzania, which is now almost the only area left in Africa where migratory wildlife systems remain. The Serengeti provides a wonderful opportunity to consider how animals evolved as part of a natural wildlife community. Almost everywhere else in Africa the increase in human population has led to the disruption or complete loss of migratory ungulate populations. African savannas have great seasonality between wet and dry seasons, and migratory ungulates were able to exploit seasonal changes by moving between areas. Species such as springbok in southern Africa, white-eared kob in the Sudan, or wildebeest in the Serengeti, had well-established migration routes to take them to different grazing areas in different seasons. But their major predators, such as lions and hyenas, were not able to travel the large distances necessary to keep up with the herds, and as a consequence predators caused relatively few deaths among these migratory antelope. Most animals died from old age, malnutrition or some other cause, and the vultures, especially the griffon vultures, evolved to exploit this food supply. Migratory ungulates were originally an important feature of the Indian subcontinent, but today in India, Europe and elsewhere in the Old World the vultures are dependent on domestic animals or small remnants of wildlife held in reserves.

A bearded vulture on a rocky ledge.

There are 15 species of Old World vultures, and perhaps the most typical and the most successful have been the seven species of griffon vulture. These are all rather similar in appearance, although they differ in size. They have a powerful and sharp bill that is well designed for slicing through meat, and long, bare necks to reach far into carcasses. There is a fluffy ruff of white feathers at the base of the neck that they can use to cover over the bare neck and keep themselves warm on a cold night. The largest species is the Himalayan griffon, at up to 26½ lb (12 kg) and with a wingspan up to 122 in (310 cm). Generally the species which live in mountainous areas are much heavier than the species which live in flat grassland areas where they cannot find such strong air currents to carry them aloft. All of the griffon vultures travel great distances searching for food, and some of them are also migratory; young European griffons, for example, fly down to Africa for the winter.

European griffon vulture.

When they find food they often collect in large numbers, and I have seen over 200 birds arrive within an hour of an animal dying. Their long necks allow them to reach far inside a carcass from only a few openings in the skin. They are often aggressive toward each other when they are feeding, and have a great variety of intimidating displays and threatening squeals and groans that they use to try and exert dominance. But feeding is a serious business, and the group eat extremely rapidly and can strip a large mammal down to a bag of skin and bones within a few hours.

An adult Cape vulture from southern Africa coming in to land. These birds nest in large colonies on cliff ledges, from where they forage over huge areas of surrounding land searching for food.

The Egyptian vulture is one of the few birds in the world which uses tools. This bird is using stones to break open an ostrich egg, so that it can feed on the contents. Birds will repeatedly pick up stones in their bills and throw them onto an egg until they eventually make a hole in the shell.

Other species of vultures are specialized in other ways. There is a group of powerfully built species with massive heads and deep bills, such as the African lappet-faced vulture and European black vulture, which seem to prefer to eat skin, sinews, tendons and other tough items. These species are suspected of occasionally killing small prey, but this is rare and most of their food is scavenged. There are also some more slightly built species, such as the African white-headed and Indian black vulture, which can also tear tough skin but which may feed more on smaller carcasses and do not always associate with the other vulture species. It seems that all these birds do not travel widely like the griffon vultures, but stay within a home range. It is unusual to see more than a few birds feeding together.

The smallest species are birds like the Egyptian and hooded vultures which have slender, thin bills. They do not have much power in the bill, but can feed in a delicate way, teasing small scraps of meat left clinging to bones. They also eat many other foods, and regularly catch small insects and other small creatures. The Egyptian vulture has a special trick, being one of the few birds that uses tools. It commonly feeds on bird eggs, and in the case of small eggs it picks the whole egg up in its bill and smashes it onto the ground so that it can feed on the contents. Ostrich eggs are too large to be given this treatment. Instead, the bird searches around for stones, which it holds high in the air in its bill before throwing them down onto the shell repeatedly, until eventually it cracks open a small hole.

The Egyptian vulture has an unusually shaped, and pointed, tail and wings. This feature is shared by the bearded vulture. This spectacular bird lives in rugged mountainous areas such as the Himalayas, Ethiopia, the Alps and the Pyrenees. It has an appearance to match the magnificence of its surroundings, with a vivid red eye-ring, a black beard and handsome ginger feathers on its chest. At one time a series of subspecies were described based on differences in the intensity of the orange color of the feathers, but we now know that the feathers themselves are actually white and the birds have to wallow in red soils to turn the plumage into the characteristic bright color. This is one of the very few examples in the whole animal kingdom of cosmetics being used to improve an animal's appearance.

The bearded vulture has a weird diet, mainly eating bones. Indeed, it is the only large animal that is known to eat bone as the main part of its diet. They swallow small bones whole, but carry larger bones in their feet high into the air and drop them repeatedly onto slabs of rock until they break into smaller fragments which can then be eaten. The acid conditions in the stomach dissolve out the mineral in the bone, and the bird feeds on the fat in the bone marrow and the protein in the bone tissue itself. But because bone is so hard, it takes a long time for the birds to digest their food, and it does seem strange that they should choose such an unappetizing diet. But feeding on bones has one great advantage. These birds live in high mountains where there is only a low density of sheep and goats that they can use for food. This means that the number of dead animals that become available each year will be very few. If they relied on meat for their food, then each carcass would only last them for a few weeks before bacteria made the meat rotten. But bones do not go 'bad' in the way that meat does, because they dehydrate, and many months after an animal has died the bones will still be available for a bearded vulture to eat. So they may have specialized on bone because it is such a durable food and is the only part of a carcass which will remain around for a long period of time.

Finally, this group of birds contains the oddest of all the vultures; the only bird of prey which has become a vegetarian. The palm-nut vulture feeds mainly on the fruits of the oil palm. At one time oil palms were found growing wild in wet forests, but the commercial establishment of plantations must have given this bird a food bonanza, and its distribution today closely matches the location of palm plantations. It has also been recorded occasionally feeding on stranded fish and a few other things, but palm fruits are its favorite food.

A palm-nut vulture – a vulture which has become vegetarian.

Condors, Vultures and Humans

It is perhaps not surprising that many human societies have associated vultures with funeral rites, the freeing of the spirit of the dead, and have imbued vultures with supernatural associations. After all, vultures feed on dead bodies and then soar high into the sky.

Human attitudes to vultures are surprisingly benign in countries where the birds are a part of everyday life. They rarely evoke the feelings of revulsion or disgust which might be the attitude of some in the west. There are sensible, practical reasons for this, especially for peoples living in desert areas, where disposal of the dead can be a serious problem. Most of the deserts of the world are rocky, and there is insufficient depth of soil for a burial. Vegetation is scarce, trees are rare, and so there is also often insufficient fuel for cremation. But some significant ritual and ceremony has to be developed to mark a death in the family, to dispose of the body and signify the entry of the spirit into the next life.

The Zoroastrian religion, which originated with the Parsi people in Persia over 3500 years ago, is the world's oldest prophetic religion and is still very much alive. Fire is the center of the religious rites. The followers regard fire as a sacred creation and believe it would be wrong to use it for cremation. They also believe the earth and water to be God's creation which should not be polluted by death, which represents evil. This makes burial unacceptable. However, they believe vultures were created by God for the specific purpose of devouring corpses, and their burial ceremonies are based on the *dakhma*, or 'Towers of Silence', where the dead are laid out for vultures. Only a few religious leaders are allowed to enter the Towers and prepare the body, and during the ceremony the relatives pray in nearby gardens in quiet and tranquil surroundings. Their ceremonies are an entirely natural and dignified way of disposing of the dead. In Mongolia and

A young Andean condor.

51

Tibet bodies are also laid out for the vultures, and a professional caste have the duties of preparing the bodies. Such burial customs probably date back to the start of human societies. Wall decorations from the archaeological site of Katal Huyuk in southern Anatolia show that human societies 8000 years ago were laying out their dead in this way for vultures to consume.

In the Americas early human societies also had complex rituals involving condors, but these do not seem to have involved using them to dispose of the dead. Instead, the birds were regarded as especially strong sources of power. This no doubt relates partly to their physical size and strength. But in addition their ability to detect death and to appear mysteriously whenever a death occurred would also have given them magical associations. They became associated with an ability to predict the future. In some Indian communities in California, shamans were members of society who intervened between humans and supernatural forces, and were important as healers and predictors of future events. Condors could act as a source of shamanistic power, perhaps appearing in a dream, or a vision, and condor feathers and other artefacts were part of the ceremonies and costume of their rituals.

Other American Indians made ceremonial use of the condor as a representation of power. This might have involved dances which impersonated the condor's spirit, perhaps using costumes made with condor feathers, or rituals in which birds were captured and ceremonies held in their honor. There is archaeological evidence of condors being given ceremonial burials. In the Andes in South America other traditions involving the Andean condor involved the capture of birds, who were paraded through the villages. Sometimes the birds were then released, or on other occasions ceremonially killed in a ritual which some believe represents the Conquistadors' domination of the Andean people, or the transfer of power from the sacrificed bird to its tormentors, but the origins of these ceremonies are obscure and probably date back to pre-Columbian days. Similar ceremonies may have occurred in

In India the white-backed vultures were once extremely common in large towns and cities, helping to dispose of animal waste at sites such as this garbage dump. However, in recent years there has been a dramatic decline in the number of these birds.

the past in California involving the sacrifice of California condors.

Vultures appear prominently in the art and culture of almost every age. The Greeks and Romans considered them to be augural birds of the first rank, and in ancient Egypt two of the goddesses of upper Egypt were vulture goddesses: Mut and Nekhbet. The body of Tutankhamun was buried with two stunning pieces of gold jewelry: a flexible gold collar on the chest, and a necklace suspended from the neck, both representations of Nekhbet with her wings unfurled. The solid gold face mask also contains a magnificent representation of a vulture head, that of Nekhbet the goddess of upper Egypt, alongside that of a cobra head, a representation of the cobra goddess Wadjet from lower Egypt. These solid gold jewels, richly encrusted with lapis lazuli, carnelian, obsidian and colored glass are among the most beautiful objects to come down to us from any ancient civilization. Such stunning images of the vulture gods were not placed on the mummy just for adornment. They were there to provide magical protection in the afterlife, and the frequent use of the image of the vulture gods not only on the mummy itself but also on the coffins, lids and tomb walls, indicates the importance and power ascribed to these gods by the ancient Egyptians.

Vultures were also often associated with success in warfare. This no doubt relates to their appearance on the battlefield to devour the corpses of the enemy. Vultures do have an uncanny ability to find fighting armies. During the Crimean war it is reported that vultures became scarce throughout the whole of northern Africa, because so many birds had flown to the Crimea to feed on dead horses and soldiers on the battlefields. The British army had to send out shooting parties to protect the wounded. So it is understandable that early civilizations came to associate the appearance of vultures with the destruction of their enemies in war. One of the earliest of monuments, the Stele of the Vultures, is a stone column erected about 4600 years ago in Mesopotamia as a victory tribute, and shows

Head of a Ruppell's griffon vulture.

the enemy dead being consumed by vultures. Similar images are frequent in such memorials from early societies.

Today some vulture species live alongside people in a mutually beneficial way. Throughout Central and South America you will find towns and villages where black vultures wander the streets and markets, perched on the house roofs, waiting on the harbor walls for the fishing boats to return and congregating enthusiastically at the local garbage dump. Humans provide them with an abundant source of food through their waste. In return the birds provide a free garbage disposal service. There has been some controversy over whether vultures pose any danger to human health. John Cooper and I carried out some experiments in which vultures were fed various disease-causing organisms, including a harmless strain of anthrax. This study showed that most bacteria will be killed in passing through the gut, probably by the highly acidic stomach, and do not appear in their feces, and so vultures may well help prevent the spread of food-poisoning or disease epidemics by eating contaminated meat and sterilizing it. It is true that they may spread disease on their feathers and feet, and carry this into towns, but under the harsh tropical conditions in which most vultures live, the exposure to the ultraviolet radiation in sunlight will quickly kill most bacteria on the skin and plumage. On balance urban vultures probably do more good than harm.

In India the white-backed vulture fills a similar role, living right in the middle of even major cities, and in West Africa, but curiously not in East Africa, the town scavenger is the hooded vulture. All these birds have undoubtedly benefited greatly from the increasing human population and the steady growth of towns and cities. Such species are now heavily dependent on humans to provide them with food. But other vulture species have not been so lucky and have not been able to adapt to man. Some vultures have become so rare that drastic conservation action is the only way we will prevent them from becoming extinct.

An Andean condor soars over the mountains.

Conservation

Vultures evolved to feed as a part of natural wildlife communities, and over the past few hundred years the growth in the human population has meant that there is less and less land available for wild animals. Many vulture species have not been able to withstand this environmental change, and their numbers have been steadily declining. Of the 22 species of vultures in the world, about a third are declining in numbers so fast that they are receiving active conservation management.

Before looking at the management methods that can be used to protect vulture species, we need to have a clear understanding of why their numbers are declining. One potential factor is that many species have had to change their feeding habits, and instead of seeking deer or antelope carcasses they have to rely on domestic cows and sheep. Maybe they just cannot find enough food? Fortunately, with vultures it is relatively easy to calculate the amount of food available to a population of birds, given the number of large mammals within their foraging range and their annual mortality rates. A number of such studies have been carried out in areas where vulture populations are falling and all of them suggest that the size of the food supply is not a problem. In fact, where vultures are feeding on domestic animals they usually find far more food than they would have done if they were eating wild animals, because pastoral farmers often keep their livestock at high densities, and mortality rates among livestock are often high.

The causes of the decline in vulture numbers usually lie elsewhere. All vultures face a common problem. They tend to be long-lived birds, and some of the larger species probably survive for 50 years or more. They live so long because in the conditions in which they evolved their natural mortality was very low, and few adult birds would die each year. They were able to keep stable numbers with a very low rate of reproduction. Most vultures have among the

The American king vulture is commonly found in dense, tropical forest.

The condors are the largest of the American vultures.
Andean condors roost at a series of caves in a rock face in Argentina (above).

lowest rates of reproduction of any birds in the world. Many of the larger species will not start breeding until they are between six and eight years old, will lay only a single egg, and the largest species, like the condors, take so long to rear a chick that they will only be able to breed every two years. If any human activities cause an increase in the number of birds which die each year, the populations are unable to respond by producing more young, and so over time their numbers will steadily decline towards extinction.

Unfortunately for the vultures, many of man's activities lead to vulture deaths. Vultures are still occasionally shot by irresponsible hunters. But the main problems come from dangers that few people are aware of. In southern Africa a considerable number of birds die in cattle drinking troughs: farmers use windpumps to provide their stock with water in concrete ponds. Vultures find these pools very useful places to bathe after feeding. Cattle troughs usually have vertical walls, and when the birds jump in to get their feathers wet they are

A pair of California condors preen.

unable to climb out and will drown. The solution is easy – to provide a small ramp at one end to allow the birds, and any other animals which fall in, to climb out to safety. Power lines pose another problem. The wingspan of some vultures is so large that they can reach the live wires while still standing on the steel frame, and so bypass the insulators. In Israel in 1982, Jossi Leshem found 43 dead griffon vultures under just three pylons – this incident killed a quarter of the total population of these vultures in northern Israel. A similar problem was found in southern Africa, where John Ledger was able to show how small changes in the design of power pylons would prevent the danger to the vultures, and save considerable financial losses to the power companies from interrupted supplies.

Because they are at the top of food chains, vultures are also at risk from accumulating pesticide residues that come from agricultural sources, which become more concentrated as they move up the food chain. In many birds of prey, pesticides can interfere with calcium metabolism and cause the birds to lay eggs which fail to hatch because they have defective eggshells. In Israel, Professor Mendelssohn considers that excessive pesticide use in the 1950s and 1960s probably contributed to the drastic fall in numbers of griffon vultures. But far more

Ruppell's griffon vulture on an elephant carcass.

serious is deliberate poisoning. In many countries it is still legal and routine to use poisons to kill animals such as wolves, coyotes, jackals, hyenas or other predators which might attack stock. In developed countries the poison should be administered in a relatively safe manner, but in countries with poorly developed pest-control programs a farmer may just lay out a carcass and deliberately scatter it with strychnine or some other deadly poison to kill anything which comes to feed. They do not intend to kill vultures, but vultures are undoubtedly killed. In South Africa in 1984 a single strychnine-poisoned cow carcass killed 42 Cape vultures. This was ten per cent of the total population of these vultures in this part of Africa, the Cape Province. At this time a survey showed that half of all farmers in South Africa routinely used strychnine for predator control. A single dead cow in Botswana was found with 79 poisoned vultures dead nearby. In 1979 one poisoned elephant carcass in Caprivi killed six lions and 150 Cape vultures. Only a few of these incidents can kill most of the vultures in an area. Because vultures collect in large numbers at a single feeding site, and come there from a considerable distance, an isolated poisoning event can have a devastating influence on vulture populations over a whole country.

White-backed vultures and spotted hyenas feed on a dead elephant. Vultures have to compete with large carnivores like lions and hyenas for their food, and their superior ability to find carcasses and consume them quickly makes vultures far more effective scavengers than any of the mammals.

The adult California condor has impressive air sacs in the throat and neck which it can inflate during courtship displays to exaggerate the colorful skin on the face and neck.

Another form of poisoning has been found to be important in the decline of the California condor. A few of these birds were found dead, or dying, with dangerously high levels of lead in their blood. It seems that the birds probably picked up the poison by feeding on the carcasses of deer or other animals that had been wounded by hunters, and contained lead fragments in their tissues.

All this may make us wonder if vultures can hope to survive in the modern world. There are indeed some people who regard birds such as the California condor as a senescent species, one that is doomed to extinction because it was part of a past era and has outlived its time. Anyone who has studied the bird would know this to be nonsense. California condors, and all other vulture species, can survive perfectly well in the modern world, if only we take some care to remove the dangers that we have placed in their way. In Europe vulture populations are now expanding, and countries like Spain have seen a spectacular increase in vulture numbers following their conservation programs.

Fortunately vultures are well suited to active conservation management. Everybody has heard of vultures, they are conspicuous, and so ideal for public education programs. One of the first and most effective has been in southern Africa, where Peter Mundy, John Ledger and many fellow enthusiasts formed the Vulture Study Group. Their energetic and imaginative publicity has changed public attitudes to vultures, informed people of the benefits of a healthy vulture population and given farmers advice on how to avoid the potential dangers that might kill birds. Conservation policies will never succeed unless they are backed by the willing support of local people.

One large advantage for vulture conservation programs compared with programs for other birds of prey is that vultures are scavengers, and so we can easily provide them with extra food. Vulture 'restaurants' were first developed in Spain, by laying out carcasses that were passed as unfit for human consumption, and the South Africans further developed the technique. Today vulture conservation programs all over the world rely on the provision of safe feeding areas. These do more than help the population through periods in the year when food may be hard to find. If the birds know that they can get a regular supply of food at one protected site, they will remain in the area. This prevents birds having to travel long distances and perhaps run the risk of encountering poison, power lines or other dangers.

A second great advantage is that most species will breed readily in captivity. Many birds of prey are difficult to breed in zoos, but vultures settle well into cages. One of the first conservation programs based on captive breeding was developed by Michel Terrasse. With very little funding, he has successfully reintroduced griffon vultures into the Massif Central region of France. In the same way the bearded vulture has been brought back to the Alps in Europe, and the California condor saved from extinction.

The California condor had been steadily declining in numbers, despite a massive field conservation effort, until by 1987 only 27 birds remained. The drastic decision was then taken to remove all the birds from the wild, and rely on captive breeding by the San Diego and Los Angeles zoos to save the species. Anyone with an interest in the conservation of endangered species should read *The California Condor; a Saga of Natural History and Conservation* by Noel and Helen Snyder. This book discusses the politics and problems of this critical conservation program, which faced enormous political difficulties as well as formidable practical and logistical challenges. Fortunately the story has a happy ending, because the dedication and skill of the team involved has quickly led to an increase in the captive population. This program has benefited from our recent advances in understanding the genetics of endangered species management, and birds are now being released back into the wild, while maintaining a sufficient breeding stock in the captive program. The world would be a much poorer place if this magnificent bird were no longer part of our environment. All of the vulture species can fill a successful and important role in the modern world if we take sufficient care to protect them.

A young Himalayan griffon vulture on a crag.

Vulture and Condor Maps and Facts

Even some of the most common species of vultures have been little studied, and we still have much to learn about their distribution and ecology. These maps are only intended to indicate likely distributions, and for many species we know little of their breeding biology.

California Condor (*Gymnogyps californianus*)

Weight: 17½-31 lb (8-14 kg).
Wingspan: about 106 in (270 cm).
Breeding: 1 egg, in cave or tree hole, incubation 55-60 days, chick fledges at about 6 months, but remains with parents for many months.

Andean Condor (*Vultur gryphus*)

Weight: Male 24-33 lb (11-15 kg), Female 18-24 lb (8-11 kg). Only American vulture with sexual dimorphism.
Wingspan: about 126 in (320 cm).
Breeding: 1 egg, in cave or rock ledge, incubation 59 days, chick fledges at about 6 months, but remains with parents for many months.

Turkey Vulture (*Cathartes aura*)

Weight: 27-64 oz (850-2000 g).
Wingspan: 71-79 in (180-200 cm).
Breeding: 2 eggs, incubation 38-41 days, chicks fledge at about 70-80 days.

Lesser Yellow-headed Vulture (*Cathartes burrovianus*)

Weight: 30-50 oz (950-1550 g).
Wingspan: about 63 in (160 cm).
Breeding: No information.

Greater Yellow-headed Vulture (*Cathartes melambrotus*)

Weight: 53 oz (1650 g).
Wingspan: Not known.
Breeding: No information.

American Black Vulture (*Coragyps atratus*)

Weight: 35-61 oz (1100-1900 g).
Wingspan: 54-59 in (137-150 cm).
Breeding: 2 eggs, on ground under trees or boulders, incubation 38-45 days, chicks fledge about 3 months.

King Vulture (*Sarcoramphus papa*)

Weight: 97-121 oz (3000-3750 g).
Wingspan: 71-78 in (180-198 cm).
Breeding: Mostly known from captive breeding: 1 egg, incubation 55-58 days, chick may fledge after about 3 months.

Egyptian Vulture (*Neophron percnopterus*)

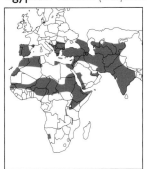

Weight: 52-71 oz (1600-2200 g).
Wingspan: 61-67 in (155-170 cm).
Breeding: 1 or 2 eggs, in caves, incubation 42 days, chicks fledge 70-85 days.

Bearded Vulture (*Gypaetus barbatus*)

Weight: 145-229 oz (4500-7100 g).
Wingspan: 98-111 in (250-282 cm).
Breeding: 1 or 2 eggs, in caves or rock ledges, incubation 53-58 days, chicks fledge 106-130 days.

Palm-nut Vulture (*Gypohierax angolensis*)

Weight: 44-55 oz (1361-1712 g).
Wingspan: 59 in (150 cm).
Breeding: 1 egg, in trees, incubation about 44 days, chicks fledge about 90 days.

Hooded Vulture *(Necrosyrtes monachus)*

Weight: 49-84 oz
(1530-2600 g).
Wingspan: 67-72 in
(170-182 cm).
Breeding: I egg, in trees,
incubation 48-54 days,
chick fledges 89-130 days.

Indian White-backed Vulture *(Gyps bengalensis)*

Weight: 113-193 oz
(3500-6000 g).
Wingspan: 81-87 in
(205-220 cm).
Breeding: I egg, in trees,
incubation about 45 days,
chicks fledge about 3
months.

African White-backed Vulture *(Gyps africanus)*

Weight: 134-232 oz
(4150-7200 g).
Wingspan: 86 in
(218 cm).
Breeding: I egg, in trees,
incubation 56 days, chicks
fledge about 4 months.

Eurasian Griffon Vulture *(Gyps fulvus)*

Weight: 13-24 lb
(6-11 kg).
Wingspan: 94-110 in
(240-280 cm).
Breeding: I egg, on rock
ledges, incubation 50-58
days, chicks fledge
110-130 days.

Cape Griffon Vulture *(Gyps coprotheres)*

Weight: 15½-24 lb
(7-11 kg).
Wingspan: 100 in
(255 cm).
Breeding: I egg, on rock
ledges, incubation 55
days, chicks fledge 140
days.

Himalayan Griffon Vulture *(Gyps himalayensis)*

Weight: 17½-26½ lb
(8-12 kg).
Wingspan: 102-122 in
(260-310 cm).
Breeding: Poorly known,
I egg, on rock ledges,
incubation about 50 days,
chicks may fledge 4 to 5
months.

Ruppell's Griffon Vulture *(Gyps rueppellii)*

Weight: 15½-20 lb (7-9 kg).
Wingspan: 94 in (240 cm).
Breeding: 1 egg, on rock ledges, incubation 55 days, chicks fledge 150 days.

Long-billed Griffon Vulture *(Gyps indicus)*

Weight: 12-13 lb (5.5-6 kg).
Wingspan: 81-90 in (205-229 cm).
Breeding: 1 egg, on rock ledges or trees, but breeding not yet studied. It is likely that there are two species of long-billed vultures in India.

Eurasian Black Vulture *(Aegypius monachus)*

Weight: 15½-27½ lb (7-12.5 kg).
Wingspan: 98½-116 in (250-295 cm).
Breeding: 1 egg, either in trees or cliffs, incubation 54-56 days, chicks fledge 95-120 days.

Lappet-faced Vulture *(Torgos tracheliotus)*

Weight: 12-21 lb (5.4-9.4 kg).
Wingspan: 110 in (280 cm).
Breeding: 1 egg, in tree nest, incubation 54-56 days, chicks fledge 125-135 days.

White-headed Vulture *(Trigonoceps occipitalis)*

Weight: 7-11½ lb (3.3-5.3 kg).
Wingspan: 90½ in (230 cm).
Breeding: 1 egg, in tree nest, incubation 55-56 days, chicks fledge 115-120 days.

Indian Red-headed Vulture *(Sarcogyps calvus)*

Weight: 116-174 oz (3600-5400 g).
Wingspan: 86-90 in (218-229 cm).
Breeding: 1 egg, in tree nest, breeding poorly known, but incubation probably about 45 days.

Index

*Entries in **bold** indicate pictures*

Recommended Reading

Del Hoyo, J., Elliott, A. & Sargatal, J. *Handbook of the Birds of the World,* Volume 2. Lynx Editions & Birdlife International, 1994.
Mundy, P., Butchart, D., Ledger, J. & Piper, S. *The Vultures of Africa.* Acorn Books and Russel Friedman Books, 1992.
Snyder, N. & H. *The California Condor: A Saga of Natural History and Conservation.* Academic Press, 2000
Wilbur, S.R., & Jackson, J.A. *Vulture Biology and Management.* University of California Press, 1983.

Biographical Note

David Houston is in the Ornithology Group at the Institute of Biomedical and Life Sciences at Glasgow University in Scotland. He has been studying vultures and the role that they play in wildlife communities for 30 years, starting with his studies for his Ph.D. at Oxford University working in the Serengeti National Park in Tanzania. He has since studied vultures in other areas of Africa, India and South America.